Contents

Introduction

Children of all ages will love these cute knitted finger puppets. They'll encourage creative play and storytelling, and are bound to become much-loved favourites in the toy box. You can choose from a variety of friendly characters and animals.

The puppets are fun and easy to make, and every project is accompanied by clear instructions describing how to achieve perfect results. You can follow them to the letter or use them as a basis for your own creations. In addition, a techniques section explains all the basic skills needed, making them suitable for experienced knitters and novices alike. Small and quick to knit, these designs are an ideal way of using up oddments of yarn and make perfect portable projects for knitters on the go. We're sure you'll enjoy making them.

Mitch Monkey

Guaranteed to raise a smile and a laugh, this mischievous little monkey will delight circus audiences with his truly amazing acrobatic antics and tricks.

MATERIALS
- 4-ply knitting yarn in buff (A), beige (B) and geranium red (C), plus small amounts of black and dark red
- Pair of 2.75mm (UK12:US2) knitting needles
- Pair of 2.25mm (UK13:US1) knitting needles
- 2 x 2.75mm (UK12:US2) double-pointed knitting needles
- 2 x 2.25mm (UK13:US1) double-pointed knitting needles
- Tapestry needle
- Polyester toy stuffing

SIZE
Mitch's body measures approx 2½in (6.25cm) in length.

TENSION
See page 40.

BODY AND HEAD
Using 2.75mm needles and A, cast on 20 sts.
Row 1: K each st tbl.
Row 2: P to end.
Row 3: K to end.
Rows 4–6: P to end.
Beg with a k row, work 20 rows in stocking stitch.
Row 27: K4, (k2tog) twice, k4, (k2tog) twice, k4 (16 sts).
Beg with a p row, work 3 rows in stocking stitch.
Row 31: K3, (inc1, k2) 3 times, inc1, k3 (20 sts).
Row 32: P to end.
Row 33: K2, (inc1, k2) 6 times (26 sts).
Beg with a p row, work 9 rows in stocking stitch.
Row 43: K2, (k2tog, k2) 6 times (20 sts).
Row 44: P to end.
Row 45: (k2tog) 10 times (10 sts).
Row 46: (P2tog) 5 times.
Cut yarn and thread through rem 5 sts.

PAWS AND ARMS
(make 2)
Using two 2.75mm double-pointed needles and A, cast on 3 sts.
Row 1: Inc1 in each st (6 sts).
Row 2: P to end.
Row 3: (K1, inc1) 3 times (9 sts).
Row 4: P to end.
Row 5: (K1, k2tog) 3 times (6 sts).
Row 6: P to end.
Row 7: (K1, k2tog) twice (4 sts); do not turn but, with RS facing, *slide sts to other end of needle and k4; rep from * 12 times more. Cast off.

EARS
(make 2)

Using 2.75mm knitting needles and A, cast on 5 sts.

Row 1: K each st tbl.
Row 2: P to end.
Row 3: K to end.
Row 4: P to end.
Row 5: K2tog, k1, k2tog (3 sts).
Row 6: P to end.
Row 7: K to end.
Row 8: P3tog; cut yarn and fasten off.

FACE

Using 2.25mm needles and B, cast on 3 sts.

Row 1: P to end.
Row 2: Inc1 in each st (6 sts).
Row 3: P to end.
Row 4: Inc1 in each st (12 sts).
Row 5: P to end.
Row 6: (K1, inc1) 6 times (18 sts).
Row 7: P to end.
Row 8: K to end. Cast off.

TAIL

Using two 2.25mm double-pointed needles and A, cast on 3 sts.

Row 1: K3; do not turn but, with RS facing, *slide sts to other end of needle and k3, rep from * 18 times more.
Cast off.

FEZ

Using a set of four 2.25mm double-pointed knitting needles and C, cast on 18 sts and divide between three needles.

Round 1: K each st tbl.
Knit 7 rounds.
Round 9: (K1, k2tog) 6 times (12 sts).
Round 10: (K2tog) 6 times (6 sts).
Round 11: (K2tog) 3 times; cut yarn and thread through rem 3 sts.

MAKING UP

Stitch hem and back seam, then stuff the head. Stitch seams on first few rows of paws and attach each to body. Stitch ears to each side of head. Stitch tail to lower edge of back. Join seam on face piece and stitch to front of head, tucking yarn ends inside. Stitch hat to top of head, adding a little stuffing if you wish.

Embroider the face: with beige yarn, stitching three vertical stitches for each eye and then a horizontal stitch for the eyebrows. Then, with black yarn, stitch a small horizontal stitch across the centre stitch of each eye and another across the top of the eye, and a small horizontal stitch for the nose. Using dark red, stitch a single straight stitch to form the mouth, couching it in place using two or three small, discreet stitches. (See page 47 for more details about embroidering facial features.)

Tilly Tiger

Is she a fearsome wild animal or someone dressed up in a cute tiger suit? You decide. Either way, Tilly is one of the most popular and well-loved performers the circus ring has ever seen.

MATERIALS
- 4-ply knitting yarn in ivory (A), tangerine (B), geranium red (C) and buttercup yellow (D), plus small amounts of peppermint and black
- Pair of 2.75mm (UK12:US2) knitting needles
- Pair of 2.25mm (UK13:US1) knitting needles
- 4 x 2.25mm (UK13:US1) double-pointed knitting needles
- Wire or plastic narrow bangle for hoop
- Tapestry needle
- Polyester toy stuffing
- Button or circle of plastic 1¾in (4.5cm) in diameter for plinth

SIZE
Tilly's body measures approx 2½in (6.25cm) in length.

TENSION
See page 40

BODY AND HEAD
Using 2.75mm needles and A, cast on 20 sts.
Row 1: K each st tbl.
Row 2: P to end.
Row 3: K to end.
Rows 4–6: P to end.
Beg with a k row, work 2 rows in stocking stitch.
Do not break off A. Join in B. Cont in stocking stitch, working (2 rows in B, then 4 rows in A) 3 times. Break off B.
Row 27: K4, (k2tog) twice, k4, (k2tog) twice, k4 (16 sts).
Beg with a p row, work 3 rows in stocking stitch.
Row 31: K3, (inc in next st, k2) 3 times, inc in next st, k3 (20 sts).
Row 32: P to end.
Row 33: K2, (inc in next st, k2) 6 times (26 sts).

Beg with a p row, work 9 rows in stocking stitch.
Row 43: K2, (k2tog, k2) 6 times (20 sts).
Row 44: P to end.
Row 45: (K2tog) 10 times.
Break off yarn and thread through rem 10 sts.

PAWS AND FRONT LEGS (make 2)
Using 2.75mm needles and A, cast on 6 sts.
Row 1: Inc in each st (12 sts).
Row 2: P to end.
Row 3: (K2tog) 6 times (6 sts).
Row 4: P to end.
Do not break off A. Join in B.
Cont in stocking stitch, working (2 rows in B, then 2 rows in A) twice.
Cast off.

TAIL

Using 2.75mm needles and A, cast on 6 sts.

Row 1: Knit.

Row 2: Purl; do not break off A. Join in B. Cont in stocking stitch, working in 2-row stripes until you have completed the 5th stripe in B, then work two further rows in B. Cast off.

EARS

(make 2)

Using 2.75mm needles and B, cast on 5 sts.

Row 1: K each st tbl.

Row 2: P to end.

Row 3: K to end.

Row 4: P to end.

Row 5: K2tog, k1, k2tog (3 sts).

Row 6: P to end.

Row 7: K3tog.

Break off yarn and fasten off.

COLLAR

Using 2.25mm needles and C, cast on 14 sts.

Row 1: K each st tbl.

Cast off knitwise.

MAKING UP THE TIGER

At base of body, fold first few rows to wrong side along purl ridge and stitch in place to create a hem. Stitch back seam of body and head. Run a length of yarn through the stitches at neckline, stuff head, and draw up yarn to close opening and shape neck. Stitch seams on paws and front legs, and attach them to body. Stitch ears to each side of head. Wrap collar around neck and stitch in place.

Join side edges of tail with a neat mattress-stitch seam, pulling up the seam slightly to cause the tail to curve, then stitch base of tail to centre back, just above hem. Embroider the face. Using peppermint yarn, stitch three horizontal stitches for each eye, then with black yarn, stitch a small vertical stitch across the centre stitch of each eye and a horizontal stitch above each eye. Embroider a nose in satin stitch

and use straight stitches to form mouth. Using B, stitch whiskers and stripes at top of head.

HOOP

Using 2.25mm needles and C, cast on 60 sts.

Row 1: K each st tbl.

Row 2: P to end.

Row 3: K to end.

Row 4: P to end.

Cast off, leaving a tail of yarn.

MAKING UP THE HOOP

Stitch the two short ends together, then wrap the knitted piece around the bangle and oversew edges together neatly.

PLINTH

This little item, shaped like a drum, is an important prop in any circus ring. It is used by Tilly when performing tricks.

Using set of four 2.25mm double-pointed needles and D, cast on 6 sts and divide stitches equally over three needles.

Round 1: Inc1 in each st (12 sts).

Round 2: K to end.

Round 3: Inc1 in each st (24 sts).

Round 4: K to end.

Round 5: (K1, inc1) 12 times (36 sts); cut B and join in C.

Round 6: Using C, k to end of round. Purl 2 rounds; cut C and rejoin D. Using B, knit 8 rounds; cut D and rejoin C.

Round 17: Using C, k to end of round. Purl 2 rounds; cut C and rejoin D.

Round 20: Using D, k to end of round.

Round 21: (K1, k2tog) 12 times (24 sts).

Round 22: K to end.

After completing round 22, insert a large button or circle cut from plastic to create a flat top for the plinth.

Round 23: (K2tog) 12 times (12 sts).

Round 24: K to end.

Round 25: (K2tog) 6 times; cut yarn and thread through rem 6 sts.

MAKING UP THE PLINTH

Before closing up the hole in the base, stuff well with polyester filling.

Using C and a long stitch, embroider zigzag pattern around side of plinth.

BALL

This two-colour ball is a useful prop for Tilly's circus tricks.

Using set of four 2.25mm double-pointed needles and D, cast on 6 sts and divide stitches equally over three needles.

Round 1: Inc1 in each st (12 sts).

Round 2: K to end of round.

Round 3: (Inc1, k1) 6 times (18 sts). Knit 4 rounds, then cut D and join in C. Using C, knit 4 rounds.

Round 12: (K2tog, k1) 6 times (12 sts).

Round 13: K to end of round.

Round 14: (K2tog) 6 times. Cut yarn and thread through rem 6 sts.

MAKING UP THE BALL

Add stuffing through gap, then pull yarn end to close up hole.

Ron Ringmaster

Overseeing the circus entertainment is an important job, and Ron, with his smart red tail coat, bow tie, top hat and dapper moustache, is ready to crack his whip and keep everything under control.

MATERIALS
- 4-ply knitting yarn in black (A), pale grey (B), turquoise (C), white (D), beige (E), geranium red (F) and chocolate (G)
- Black embroidery thread
- 1 small red button
- Button or circle of plastic approx. 1in (2.5cm) in diameter
- Pair of 2.75mm (UK12:US2) knitting needles
- 2 x 2.75mm (UK12:US2) double-pointed knitting needles
- 4 x 2.25mm (UK13:US1) double-pointed knitting needles
- Tapestry needle
- Plastic drinking straw

SIZE
Ron's body measures approx 2½in (6.25cm) in length.

TENSION
See page 40.

TROUSERS
Using two 2.75mm double-pointed needles and A, cast on 10 sts; do not cut A, but slide sts to other end of needle and join in B.

Row 1: Using B, k to end; do not cut B, but turn work and pick up A.

Row 2: Using A, p to end; do not cut A, but slide sts to other end of needle and pick up B.

Row 3: Using B, p to end; turn.

Continue in this way, working single rows in alternate colours until 35 rows have been worked, ending with a row in B.

Cast off using A.

Cut B; using A, and with RS facing, pick up and k24 sts along one long edge of work. Knit 2 rows and cast off knitwise; cut yarn and fasten off.

CUMMERBUND, TORSO AND HEAD

Cummerbund
On opposite edge of trousers, using 2.75mm needles and C, and with RS facing, pick up and k24 sts.
Knit 3 rows, cut yarn.

Torso and head
Using D, beg with a k row, work 8 rows in stocking stitch.

Row 12: K1, k2tog, (k2, k2tog) 5 times, k1 (18 sts).

Row 13: P to end; cut yarn and join in E.

Row 14: Using E, k to end.

Row 15: P to end.

Row 16: K1, inc1, (k2, inc1) 5 times, k1 (24 sts).

Beg with a p row, work 11 rows in stocking stitch.

Row 28: (K2tog) 12 times (12 sts).
Row 29: (P2tog) 6 times.
Cut yarn and thread through rem 6 sts.

ARMS
(make 2)

Using 2.75mm needles and E, cast on 4 sts.

Row 1: K to end.
Row 2: P to end.
Row 3: Inc1 in each st (8 sts).
Row 4: P to end.
Row 5: K to end.
Row 6: P to end; cut E and join in D.
Rows 7–9: Using D, k to end.
Beg with a p row, work 19 rows in stocking stitch. Cast off.

JACKET
Main part

Using 2.75mm needles and F, cast on 28 sts.

Row 1 (WS): K each st tbl.
Row 2: K to end.
Row 3: K1, p to last st, k1.
Rep rows 2 and 3 eight times more.
Row 20: K4, [(k2tog) twice, k4] 3 times (22 sts).
Row 21: P to end.
Row 22: (K2tog) 11 times (11 sts).
Row 23: P to end.
Cast off.

SLEEVES
(make 2)

Using 2.75mm needles and F, cast on 11 sts.

Row 1 (WS): K each st tbl.
Row 2: K to end.
Beg with a p row, work 11 rows in stocking stitch.
Row 14: K1, sl1, k1, psso, k5, k2tog, k1 (9 sts).
Row 15: P to end.
Row 16: K1, sl1, k1, psso, k3, k2tog, k1 (7 sts).
Row 17: P to end.
Cast off.

HAT

Using 2.25mm needles and A, cast on 1 st and k into front, back and front of this st (3 sts).

Row 1: Inc1 in each st (6 sts).
Row 2: P to end.
Row 3: Inc1 in each st (12 sts).
Row 4: P to end.
Row 5: Inc1 in each st (24 sts).
Beg with a p row, work 11 rows in stocking stitch.
Row 17: (K1, inc1) 12 times (36 sts).
Row 18: P to end.
Row 19: (K2, inc1) 12 times (48 sts).
Row 20: P to end.
Cast off.

BOW TIE

Using 2.25mm needles and A, cast on 11 sts.

Row 1: K each st tbl.
Row 2: P to end.
Row 3: K to end.
Cast off knitwise.

WHIP

Using 2.25mm needles and G, cast on 28 sts.

Row 1: K each st tbl.
Knit 2 rows.
Cast off.

MAKING UP

Stitch back seam of trousers, torso and head. Run a length of yarn through the stitches at neckline, stuff head and draw up yarn to close opening and shape neck. Wrap jacket around body, placing the two side edges at centre front. Stitch edges together about ½in (1cm) down from cast-off edge and stitch button on top of this join. Fold back edges above this point and stitch in place to form lapels.

Stitch arm seams, stuffing with any remaining yarn ends, then fold over approximately ½in (1cm) at top of each, to create extra bulk; attach to top of main piece of jacket at shoulders. Stitch sleeve seams, slip each over one of the arms and stitch to jacket.

Using yarn E, make ears from bullion stitch and oversew the central line of stitches to form a nose. Use black embroidery thread to embroider eyes, eyebrows, a moustache and small mouth. (See page 47 for more details about embroidering facial features.) Stitch the seam on the hat, place button in top of hat and stuff, then stitch the hat to top of the head.

To make the bow tie, fold under ¼in (6mm) on each short edge, then bind tail of yarn two or three times around centre to form a bow shape. Stitch to front of neck. To make up the whip, cut a 3in (7.5cm) length from a narrow plastic drinking straw, wrap the strip of knitting around it and oversew cast-on and cast-off edges together. Tuck in end, leaving one yarn end dangling. Fold one of the ringmaster's hands over the whip handle and stitch in place.

Charlie Clown

No circus is complete without a clown to entertain
the crowds, and this one, with his bright costume, funny hat
and big red nose, fits the bill perfectly.

MATERIALS
- 4-ply knitting yarn in geranium red (A), banana (B), Prussian blue (C), white (D), pale peach (E), tangerine (F), turquoise (G), ivory (H), plus small amount of black
- 2 small white buttons
- Pair of 2.75mm (UK12:US2) knitting needles
- Pair of 2.25mm (UK13:US1) knitting needles
- 4 x 2.25mm (UK13:US1) double-pointed knitting needles
- Tapestry needle
- Polyester toy filling

SIZE
Charlie's body measures approx 3in (7.5cm) in length.

TENSION
See page 40.

TROUSERS
Using 2.75mm needles and A, cast on 12 sts.
Row 1: K each st tbl.
Row 2: P to end; do not cut A, but join in B.
Row 3: Using B, k to end.
Row 4: P to end.
Row 5: Using A, k to end.
Row 6: P to end.
Rep rows 3 to 6 eight times more; cast off and cut B.

Hem
Using 2.75mm needles and A, with RS of trousers facing, pick up and k22 sts, evenly spaced, along one long edge.
Row 1: P to end.
Cast off knitwise.

BELT
Using 2.75mm needles and C, with RS of trousers facing, pick up and k20 sts along opposite long edge.
Beg with a p row, work 6 rows in stocking stitch.
Cast off purlwise.

TORSO AND HEAD
Using 2.75mm needles and B, cast on 20 sts.
Beg with a k row, work 12 rows in stocking stitch.
Row 13: K4, (k2tog) twice, k4, (k2tog) twice, k4 (16 sts).
Row 14: P to end; cut B and join in D.
Row 15: Using D, k4, (inc1 in next st) twice, k4, (inc1 in next st) twice, k4 (20 sts).

Beg with a p row, work 9 rows in stocking stitch.

Row 25: K1, (k2tog, k2) 4 times, k2tog, k1 (15 sts).

Row 26: (P1, p2tog) 5 times (10 sts).

Row 27: (K2tog) 5 times; cut yarn and thread through rem 5 sts.

ARMS
(make 2)

Using 2.75mm needles and E, cast on 4 sts.

Row 1: Inc1 in each st (8 sts).

Row 2: P to end.

Beg with a p row, work 3 rows in stocking stitch; cut E and join in A.

Using A, work 2 rows in stocking stitch; cut A and join in B.

Using B, work 10 rows in stocking stitch. Cast off.

BRACES
(make 2)

Using 2.25mm needles and F, cast on 25 sts.

Row 1: K each st tbl.

Row 2: P to end.

Row 3: K to end.

Cast off knitwise.

HAT
(in two pieces)

Crown

Using 2.25mm needles and G, cast on 1 st and k into front, back, front, back and front of this st (5 sts).

Row 1: Inc1 in each st (10 sts).

Row 2: P to end.

Row 3: (K1, inc1) 5 times (15 sts).

Row 4: P to end.

Row 5: (K2, inc1) 5 times (20 sts).

Row 6: P to end.

Row 7: (K3, inc1) 5 times (25 sts).

Row 8: P to end.

Row 9: K to end.

Cast off knitwise.

Brim

Using 2.25mm needles and G, cast on 5 sts.

Knit 68 rows.

Cast off.

RUFF

Using 2.25mm needles and H, *cast on 6 sts using cable method, cast off 3 sts; rep from * 9 times more (30 sts); turn.

Row 1: K to end.

Cast off all sts and cut yarn, leaving a long tail.

Thread the tail of yarn in and out of sts on cast-off edge.

NOSE

Using 2.25mm needles and A, cast on 6 sts.

Beg with a k row, work 8 rows in stocking stitch.

Cast off.

MAKING UP THE CLOWN

Fold belt over and stitch cast-off edge to top of trousers, then, with right sides together, stitch up the back seam using backstitch; turn right sides out. Stitch back seam of torso and head in the same way. Run a length of yarn through the stitches at neckline, stuff head, and draw up yarn to close opening and shape neck.

Stitch arm seams, stuffing with any remaining yarn ends, then attach to body at shoulders. Stitch trousers to bottom edge of torso. Stitch one end of each of the braces to the back of the belt, cross the two pieces over at centre back and stitch to belt at front. Stitch buttons to ends of braces. Place ruff over head and pull up yarn end to fit neck, then secure with a few stitches.

Using one of the yarn ends on the nose, stitch a running stitch all around edge and pull up tight. With purl stitches as RS, stuff the nose with a tiny wisp of polyester filling or with a scrap of yarn, then stitch to centre of face. Using yarn A, embroider mouth, and make ears using bullion stitch, then

use a little black yarn to embroider eyes and eyebrows. (See page 47 for more details about embroidering facial features.)

Stitch seam on crown of hat and stitch to top of head, then stitch two short ends of hat brim together, run a gathering stitch around one long edge and pull up to fit head; stitch in place around bottom edge of crown.

Ring mat
(made in one piece)

This colourful ring mat matches the plinth on page 7 and provides an ideal performance area for all the circus folk.

Using set of four 2.25mm double-pointed needles and B, cast on 6 sts and divide equally between over needles.

Round 1: Inc1 in each st (12 sts).

Round 2 and each even-numbered round: K to end of round.

Round 3: (Inc1, k1) 6 times (18 sts).

Round 5: (Inc1, k2) 6 times (24 sts).

Round 7: (Inc1, k3) 6 times (30 sts)

Round 9: (Inc1, k4) 6 times (36 sts).

Round 11: (Inc1, k5) 6 times (42 sts).

Round 13: (Inc1, k6) 6 times (48 sts).

Round 15: (Inc1, k7) 6 times (54 sts).

Round 17: (Inc1, k8) 6 times (60 sts).

Round 19: (Inc1, k9) 6 times (66 sts); cut B and join in A.

Round 20: Using A, k to end.

Round 21: (Inc1, k10) 6 times (72 sts).

Round 23: (Inc1, k11) 6 times (78 sts).

Cast off.

MAKING UP THE RING MAT

Weave in yarn ends on WS of work; press under a damp cloth.

Spud Scarecrow

This smiling scarecrow looks too cheerful to frighten the birds,
but when it comes to storytelling and play-acting, he will be
a welcome participant in any farmyard tale.

MATERIALS
- 4-ply knitting yarn in chocolate (A), mustard (B), olive green (C) and geranium red (D), plus a small amount of buttercup yellow and black
- 1 small brown button
- Pair of 2.75mm (UK12:US2) knitting needles
- Pair of 2.25mm (UK13:US1) knitting needles
- Tapestry needle
- Polyester toy stuffing
- Plastic drinking straw

SIZE
Spud's body measures approx 2½in (6.25cm) in length.

TENSION
See page 40.

BODY AND HEAD
(made in one piece)
Using 2.75mm needles and A, cast on 24 sts.

Row 1: K to end.

Row 2: P to end.

Rows 3–4: K to end.

Row 5: (K1, p1) 12 times.
Rep the last row 25 times more.

Row 31: (K2, k2tog) 6 times (18 sts); cut A and join in B.

Row 32: Using B, p to end.

Row 33: K to end.

Row 34: P to end.

Row 35: K6, (inc1 in next st) 6 times, k6 (24 sts).
Beg with a p row, work 11 rows in stocking stitch.

Row 47: (K2tog) 12 times (12 sts).

Row 48: (P2tog) 6 times; cut yarn and thread through rem 6 sts.

TWIG ARMS
Using 2.25mm needles and A, cast on 22 sts.

Row 1: K each st tbl.
Knit 2 rows.
Cast off.

JACKET

Main part
Using 2.75mm needles and C, cast on 30 sts.
Knit 2 rows.

Row 3: K to end.

Row 4: P to end.
Rep rows 3 and 4 eight times more.

Row 21: K5, [(k2tog) twice, k4] 3 times, k1 (24 sts).
Row 22: K to end.
Row 23: (K2tog) 12 times (12 sts).
Row 24: P to end.
Cast off knitwise.

Sleeves
(make 2)
Using 2.75mm needles and C, cast on 10 sts.
Knit 3 rows.
Beg with a p row, work 17 rows in stocking stitch.
Cast off.

Collar
Using 2.75mm needles and C, cast on 12 sts.
Row 1: K to end.
Row 2: Inc1 in first st, k10, inc1 in last st (14 sts).
Cast off.

HAT
Using 2.75mm needles and A, cast on 6 sts.
Row 1: Inc1 in each st (12 sts).
Row 2: K to end.
Row 3: Inc1 in each st (24 sts).
Knit 11 rows.
Row 15: (K1, inc1) 12 times (36 sts).
Row 16: K to end.
Row 17: (K2, inc1) 12 times (48 sts).
Row 18: K to end.
Cast off knitwise.

SCARF
Using 2.25mm needles and D, cast on 36 sts, then cast off.

FLOWER
Using 2.25mm needles and D, cast on 8 sts, cut yarn, leaving a tail. Thread this on to a tapestry needle, then take through each st in turn, starting with the first st of the row, forming a ring. Draw up, not too tightly, to form a rosette with the stitch loops forming petals.

MAKING UP
Stitch back seam of body and head.
Run a length of yarn through the stitches at neckline, stuff head, and draw up yarn to close opening and shape neck. Fold first few rows of body along ridge on row 4 to outside and stitch in place.

Wrap jacket around body, placing the two side edges at centre front. Stitch edges together about ½in (1cm) down from cast-off edge and stitch button on top of this join. Fold back edges above this point and stitch in place to form lapels, then stitch cast-on edge of collar in place on top edge of jacket, around back of neck; stitch collar points to front of jacket, above lapels. To make pocket flaps, pick up and k4 sts on one side of jacket, using yarn C, then cast off; do the same on the other side.

To make up the twig arms, cut two 2in (5cm) lengths from a narrow plastic drinking straw, wrap a strip of knitting around each, and oversew cast-on and cast-off edges together. Attach to top of main piece of jacket at shoulders. Make two bundles of short lengths of buttercup-yellow yarn and stitch around ends of arms. Trim ends of yarn. Stitch sleeve seams, slip one over each of the arms and stitch to jacket at shoulders.

Stitch the seam on the hat and then the hat to the top of the head. Stitch flower to side of hat. Using buttercup-yellow yarn, make a centre to the flower using satin stitch. Using C, embroider a leaf at each side of the flower using a lazy daisy stitch.

Use black yarn to embroider eyes in satin stitch, and a smiling mouth by stitching a line of running stitches, then a row of vertical stitches along this line. Knot scarf around neck.

Henrietta Hen

Practise your clucks and squawks: here comes the cheeky little hen known as 'Rietta', strutting around the farmyard, pecking at niblets of corn and the occasional tasty worm.

MATERIALS

- 4-ply knitting yarn in banana yellow (A), tangerine (B) and geranium red (C), plus a small amount of black
- Pair of 2.75mm (UK12:US2) knitting needles
- Pair of 2.25mm (UK13:US1) knitting needles
- Tapestry needle
- Polyester toy stuffing

SIZE

Henrietta's body measures approx 2in (5cm) in length.

TENSION

See page 40.

BODY

Using 2.75mm needles and A, cast on 20 sts.

Row 1: K each st tbl.
Row 2: P to end.
Row 3: K to end.
Row 4: P to end.
Row 5: K1, (yfwd, k2tog) 9 times, k1.
Beg with a p row, work 19 rows in stocking stitch.
Row 25: (K3, k2tog) 4 times (16 sts).
Row 26: (P2, p2tog) 4 times (12 sts).
Row 27: (K1, k2tog) 4 times (8 sts).
Row 28: (P2, p2tog) twice.
Cut yarn and thread through rem 6 sts.

HEAD

Using 2.75mm needles and A, cast on 24 sts.

Row 1: K each st tbl.
Row 2: P to end.

Row 3: K to end.
Row 4: P to end.
Row 5: K1, (yfwd, k2tog) 11 times, k1.
Beg with a p row, work 5 rows in stocking stitch.
Row 11: K1, (k2tog, k2) 5 times, k2tog, k1 (18 sts).
Row 12: P to end.
Row 13: (K1, k2tog) 6 times (12 sts).
Row 14: (P2tog) 6 times (6 sts).
Row 15: (Inc1) 6 times (12 sts).
Row 16: P to end.
Row 17: K1, (inc1, k2) 3 times, inc1, k1 (16 sts).
Beg with a p row, work 10 rows in stocking stitch.
Row 28: (P2tog) 8 times (8 sts).
Row 29: (K2tog) 4 times.
Cut yarn and thread through rem 4 sts.

WINGS
(make 2)
Using 2.75mm needles and A, cast on
1 st.

Row 1: Inc2 (k into front, back and front
of st) (3 sts).
Row 2: P to end.
Row 3: K1, inc2, k1 (5 sts).
Row 4: P to end.
Row 5: (K1, inc1) twice, k1 (7 sts).
Row 6: P to end.
Row 7: K1, inc1, k3, inc1, k1 (9 sts).
Beg with a p row, work 10 rows in
stocking stitch.
Row 18: (P2tog) twice, p1, (p2tog) twice;
cut yarn and thread through rem 5 sts.

BEAK
Using 2.75mm needles and B, cast on
6 sts.

Row 1: K each st tbl.
Row 2: P to end.
Row 3: (K2tog) 3 times (3 sts).
Row 4: P3tog; fasten off.

WATTLE
Using 2.75mm needles and C, cast on
9 sts.
Cast off.

COMB
Using 2.25mm needles and C, (cast
on 4 sts, cast off 3 sts, return st on RH
needle to LH needle) 3 times (3 sts).
Row 1: Knit each st tbl.
Cast off.

MAKING UP
Stitch back seam of body. Do the same
with the head. Use yarn ends to neaten the
wing tips, then fold each wing in half (but
do not stitch edges together) and attach
wings to body, with cast-off edges at each
side of base of neck. Stuff head with
polyester filling, then place on top of body
and wings; stitch firmly in place.

Fold beak in half and stitch sides together
to form a tight cone, then attach to centre
front of head. Fold wattle in half and
oversew edges, then stitch in place below
beak. Stitch comb to top of head.
Embroider eyes using black yarn.

Priscilla Pig

Every farmyard needs a pig to eat up the food scraps.
This little pink piggy has a body constructed in two layers
with padding in between to give her a plump shape.

MATERIALS
- 4-ply knitting yarn in pink (A)
- Small amount of black yarn
- Pair of 2.75mm (UK12:US2) knitting needles
- Tapestry needle
- Polyester toy stuffing

SIZE
Priscilla's body measures approx 2½in (6.25cm) in length.

TENSION
See page 40.

BODY AND HEAD
Using 2.75mm needles and A, cast on 5 sts.
Row 1: Inc1 in each st (10 sts).
Row 2: P to end.
Row 3: Inc1 in each st (20 sts).
Beg with a p row, work 24 rows in stocking stitch.
Row 28: K to end.
Row 29: K2, (inc1 in next st, k4) 3 times, inc1, k2 (24 sts).
Row 30: P to end.
Row 31: K2, inc1, k5, inc1, k6, inc1, k5, inc1, k2 (28 sts).
Row 32: P to end.
Row 33: K2, inc1, k6, inc1, k8, inc1, k6, inc1, k2 (32 sts).
Beg with a p row, work 21 rows in stocking stitch.
Row 55: (K2tog, k2) 4 times, (k2, k2tog) 4 times (24 sts).

Row 56: P to end.
Row 57: (K2tog) 12 times (12 sts).
Row 58: P to end.
Row 59: Inc1 in each st (24 sts).
Beg with a p row, work 9 rows in stocking stitch.
Row 69: (K2tog) 12 times (12 sts).
Row 70: P to end.
Row 71: (K2tog) 6 times.
Cut yarn and thread through rem 6 sts.

TROTTERS
(make 2)
Using 2.75mm needles and A, cast on 4 sts.
Row 1: Inc1 in each st (8 sts).
Beg with a p row, work 7 rows in stocking stitch.
Cast off.

EARS
(make 2)
Using 2.75mm knitting needles and A, cast on 1 st.

Row 1: Inc1 (2 sts).
Row 2: P to end.
Row 3: Inc1 in each st (4 sts).
Row 4: P to end.
Row 5: Inc1, k2, inc1 (6 sts).
Beg with a p row, work 5 rows in stocking stitch.
Cast off.

SNOUT
Using 2.75mm needles and A, cast on 16 sts.

Row 1: K each st tbl.
Row 2: P to end.
Rows 3–5: K to end.
Row 6: P to end.
Row 7: K to end.
Cast off knitwise.

TAIL
Using 2.75mm knitting needles and A, cast on 25 sts.

Cast-off row: K1,* k2tog, slip first st on RH needle over 2nd st, rep from * until 1 st remains; fasten off.

MAKING UP
With right sides together, stitch the sides with a neat backstitch seam, leaving a gap near base of body close to the garter-stitch ridge. Turn right sides out and, inserting stuffing into gap in seam, stuff head and the space between the inner and outer body parts. Stitch the seam closed using mattress stitch on the right side of work. Sew a running stitch around neckline and pull up to tighten slightly, then attach the top of the inner part of the body to the neck with a few discreet stitches.

To form the snout, fold the knitted piece in half along the garter-stitch ridge, right sides out, and roll up tightly, holding it in place with a few stitches, then stitch to front of head. Fold the tail, oversewing the long edges together tightly and leaving about ¼in (6mm) at one end unstitched. Stitch this flat end to centre back, just above hem.

Fold each trotter in half lengthways and stitch, then attach to sides of body, about ¾in (1.5cm) below neckline. Stitch ears in place at each side of head. Use black yarn to embroider eyes and nostrils.

Dennis Duck

Dennis is a friendly duck. He is happy to swim around the duckpond or snooze in the shade of a haystack, and he is always ready and willing to take part in your storytelling.

MATERIALS
- 4-ply knitting yarn in white (A) and tangerine (B), plus a small amount of black
- Pair of 2.75mm (UK12:US2) knitting needles
- 2 x double-pointed 2.75mm (UK12:US2) knitting needles
- Tapestry needle
- Polyester toy stuffing
- Short length of plastic drinking straw

SIZE
Dennis's body measures approx 2¼in (5.5cm) in length.

TENSION
See page 40.

BODY AND HEAD
Using 2.75mm needles and A, cast on 20 sts.
Row 1: K each st tbl.
Row 2: P to end.
Row 3: K to end.
Row 4: P to end.
Row 5: P to end.
Beg with a p row, work 19 rows in stocking stitch.
Row 25: (K3, k2tog) 4 times (16 sts).
Row 26: (P2, p2tog) 4 times (12 sts).
Row 27: (K1, k2tog) 4 times (8 sts).
Row 28: (P2, p2tog) twice (6 sts).
Beg with a k row, work 6 rows in stocking stitch for neck.
Row 35: (Inc1) 6 times (12 sts).
Row 36: P to end.
Row 37: (K1, inc1) 6 times (18 sts).

Beg with a p row, work 5 rows in stocking stitch.
Row 43: (K1, k2tog) 6 times (12 sts).
Row 44: P to end.
Row 45: (K2tog) 6 times (6 sts).
Row 46: (P2 tog) 3 times; cut yarn and thread through rem 3 sts.

WINGS
(make 2)
Using 2.75mm needles and A, cast on 1 st.
Row 1: Inc2 (k into front, back and front of st) (3 sts).
Row 2: P to end.
Row 3: K1, inc2, k1 (5 sts).
Row 4: P to end.
Row 5: (K1, inc1) twice, k1 (7 sts).
Row 6: P to end.

Row 7: K1, inc1, k3, inc1, k1 (9 sts).
Beg with a p row, work 10 rows in
stocking stitch.
Row 18: (P2tog) twice, p1, (p2tog) twice;
cut yarn and thread through rem 5 sts.

BEAK

Using 2.75mm needles and B, cast on 1 st.
Row 1: Inc2 (3 sts).
Row 2: P to end.
Row 3: K1, inc2, k1 (5 sts).
Beg with a p row, work 4 rows in
stocking stitch.

Row 8: P2tog, p1, p2tog (3 sts).
Row 9: K to end.
Row 10: P to end.
Row 11: K1, inc2, k1 (5 sts).
Beg with a p row, work 5 rows in
stocking stitch.
Cast off.

MAKING UP

Stitch back seam of body and head.
Stuff head with polyester filling, then
insert a short length of plastic drinking
straw into neck. Stitch a few discreet
stitches across base of neck to hold the
straw in place.

Attach wings to body, at each side of base
of neck. Use yarn ends to neaten the wing
tip. Fold beak in half at narrowest point and
stitch sides together by oversewing, then
attach to centre front of head.

Make a small bundle of yarn A and stitch to
top of head, then trim to form a short tuft.
Embroider eyes using black yarn.

Freddie Frog

Most people will see this frog simply as a pond-dwelling amphibian, but any passing princesses will view him as a potential husband and kiss him in the hope of a magical transformation.

MATERIALS
- 4-ply knitting yarn in sage green (A) and white (B), plus small amounts of black and red
- Pair of 2.75mm (UK12:US2) knitting needles
- 2 x double-pointed 2.75mm (UK12:US2) knitting needles
- Tapestry needle
- Polyester toy filling

SIZE
Freddie Frog measures approx 2½in (6.25cm) in length.

TENSION
See page 40.

BODY AND HEAD
Using 2.75mm needles and A, cast on 24 sts.

Row 1: K each st tbl.

Knit 27 rows.

Row 29: K3, (k3tog, k2) 3 times, k3tog, k3 (16 sts).

Knit 3 rows.

Row 33: K3, (inc1 in next st, k2) 3 times, inc1 in next st, k3 (20 sts).

Row 34: K2, (inc1 in next st, k2) 6 times (26 sts).

Row 35: K to end.

Row 36: K2, (inc1 in next st, k6) 3 times, inc1 in next st, k2 (30 sts).

Knit 4 rows.

Row 41: K2, (k2tog, k4) 4 times, k2tog, k2 (25 sts).

Row 42: K to end.

Row 43: K1, (k2tog, k5) 3 times, k2tog, k1 (21 sts).

Row 44: K to end.

Row 45: K2, (k2tog, k3) 3 times, k2tog, k2 (17 sts).

Row 46: K3, (k2tog, k1) 3 times, k2tog, k3 (13 sts).

Row 47: K2, (k3tog) 3 times, k2.

Cut yarn, leaving a tail, and thread through rem 7 sts.

ARMS AND HANDS
(make 2)
Using 2.75mm needles and A, cast on 16 sts.

Row 1: K each st tbl.

Hand
(Turn and cast on 8 sts; turn and cast off 8 sts) 3 times; cast off rem sts.

EYES
Using two 2.75mm double-pointed needles and A, cast on 5 sts.

Row 1: K5, do not turn, but slide sts to other end of needle.
Rep this row 39 times more, cast off.

EYEBALLS
(make 2)
Using 2.75mm needles and B, cast on 16 sts, cast off.

MAKING UP
Stitch back seam of body and head. Stuff head with polyester filling. Stitch a running stitch around neckline and pull up tightly.

Attach arms to body, just below head. Use yarn end between 'fingers' to neaten the hand, gathering up the stitches that form each finger so that they are more rigid.

To create the eyes, stitch centre of cord to centre top of head, then roll up each end towards centre and secure with a few firm stitches. Curl the whites of the eyes into circles and stitch in place. Thread a tapestry needle with black yarn and embroider pupils in satin stitch. Thread needle with red yarn and embroider one long horizontal stitch across centre of face for mouth, then oversew with couching stitches to create a wide mouth. Embroider nostrils using black yarn. (See page 47 for more details about embroidering facial features.)

Wilma Witch

Every story needs its villain – and that's where Wilma makes her dramatic entrance. With her scary face and magic broomstick, she is the mean and nasty member of the group.

MATERIALS
- 4-ply knitting yarn in black (A), apple green (B), purple (C), plum (D), chocolate (E) and mustard (F), plus small amounts of grey and red
- Pair of 2.75mm (UK12:US2) knitting needles
- Pair of 2.25mm (UK13:US1) knitting needles
- Narrow plastic drinking straw
- Tapestry needle
- Polyester toy stuffing

SIZE
- Wilma's body measures approx 2½in (6.25cm) in length

TENSION
See page 40

SPECIAL ABBREVIATIONS
- MB1: increase by knitting into front, back, front, back and front of stitch, turn and p5; turn and k5; turn and p5; turn and pass second, third, fourth and fifth st over first st, then k into the back of this st.
- MB2: increase by knitting into front, back and front of st, turn and p3, turn and pass second and third sts over first st, then k into the back of this st.

BODY AND HEAD
Using 2.75mm needles and A, cast on 20 sts.
Row 1: K each st tbl.
Row 2: P to end.
Row 3: K to end.
Row 4: P to end.
Row 5: K1, (yfwd, k2tog) 9 times, k1.
Beg with a p row, work 23 rows in stocking stitch.
Row 29: K4, [(k2tog) twice, k4] twice (16 sts).
Row 30: P to end; cut A and join in B.
Row 31: Using B, k to end.
Row 32: P to end.
Row 33: K6, (inc1 in next st) 4 times, k6 (20 sts).
Row 34: P to end.
Row 35: K10, pick up loop in front of next st and MB1, k10 (21 sts).
Row 36: P to end.
Row 37: K to end.

Row 38: P to end.
Row 39: K10, MB2 in next st, k10.
Row 40: P to end.
Beg with a k row, work 4 rows in stocking stitch.
Row 45: (K2tog) 5 times, k1, (k2tog) 5 times (11 sts).
Row 46: (P2tog) twice, p3tog, (p2tog) twice; cut yarn and thread through rem 5 sts.

SKIRT
Using 2.75mm needles and C, cast on 40 sts.
Row 1: K each st tbl.
Row 2: P to end.
Row 3: K to end.
Row 4: P to end.
Row 5: K1, (yfwd, k2tog) 19 times, k1.
Beg with a p row, work 13 rows in stocking stitch.
Row 19: (K2tog) 20 times (20 sts).

Row 20: P to end.
Row 21: K to end.
Cast off knitwise.

ARMS AND SLEEVES
(make 2)
Using 2.75mm needles and B, cast on 4 sts.
Row 1: K each st tbl.
Row 2: Inc1 in each st (8 sts).
Beg with a p row, work 3 rows in stocking stitch; cut B and join in C.
Row 6: Using C, cast on 4 sts, k to end (12 sts).
Row 7: Cast on 4 sts, k to end (16 sts).
Beg with a k row, continue in stocking stitch for 16 rows, decreasing 1 st at each end of seventh, eleventh and fifteenth rows (10 sts). Cast off.

SHAWL
Using 2.25mm needles and D, cast on 1 st.
Row 1: K into front, back and front of this st (3 sts).
Cont in garter stitch (k every row), inc 1 st at each end of every row until there are 29 sts. Cast off.

HAT
Using 2.75mm needles and A, cast on 22 sts.
Row 1: K each st tbl.
Row 2: P to end.
Row 3: K1, k2tog, k to last 3 sts, k2tog, k1 (20 sts).
Rep rows 2 and 3 until 6 sts remain.
Next row: P to end.
Next row: (K2tog) 3 times (3 sts).
Next row: P to end.
Next row: K3tog; fasten off.

Hat brim
Using 2.25mm needles and A, cast on 4 sts.
Knit 68 rows. Cast off.

MAKING UP THE WITCH
At base of body, fold first few rows to wrong side along eyelet row and stitch in place to create a picot hem. Stitch back seam of body and head. Run a length of yarn through the stitches at neckline, stuff head and draw up yarn to close opening and shape neck.

At base of skirt, fold first few rows to wrong side along eyelet row and stitch in place to create a picot hem. Stitch back seam of skirt; run a length of yarn through the stitches at waistline, slip on to body and stitch top of skirt to body at waistline, pulling up yarn to tighten top of skirt slightly. Stitch seams on each arm and sleeve piece, adding a little stuffing to sleeves if you wish; stitch tops of sleeves to sides of body.

Place centre of cast-off edge of shawl at centre back of neck, then bring ends of shawl to front, cross over and stitch in place. Cut strands of grey yarn, lay them across the top of the head and stitch in place down centre, using matching yarn and backstitch.

Stitch seam on hat and stitch to top of head, then stitch two short ends of hat brim together, run a gathering stitch around one long edge and pull up to fit head; stitch in place around bottom edge of hat.

To create the crinkly effect on the hair, use the point of the tapestry needle to separate the strands of grey yarn, running the needle from the top of each strand, where it emerges from the hat brim, to the tip. Trim yarn ends to the desired length.

Neaten and shape the chin using matching yarn. Use black yarn to embroider eyes and eyebrows. For the mouth, stitch two horizontal stitches in crimson, then one horizontal stitch in black between the two. (See page 47 for more details about embroidering facial features.)

BROOMSTICK
This is an essential piece of kit for any witch, allowing her to fly through the air.

Using 2.25mm knitting needles and E, cast on 28 sts.

Row 1: K each st tbl.
Knit 2 rows. Cast off.

MAKING UP THE BROOMSTICK
Cut a 3¼in (8cm) length from a narrow plastic drinking straw, wrap the strip of knitting around it and oversew cast-on and cast-off edges together. Bind short lengths of yarn F around one end for the bristles.

Princess Clarissa

In her pretty pink dress and golden crown, this beautiful princess
can help you to act out all kinds of favourite fairy stories
– and there is sure to be a happy ending.

MATERIALS
- 4-ply knitting yarn in white (A), pale peach (B), pink (C), buttercup yellow (D) and gold (E), plus small amount of blue
- Embroidery thread in black
- 1 fancy button
- Pair of 2.75mm (UK12:US2) knitting needles
- Pair of 2.25mm (UK13:US1) knitting needles
- Tapestry needle
- Polyester toy stuffing

SIZE
Princess Clarissa's body measures approximately 2½in (6.25cm) in length.

TENSION
See page 40.

BODY AND HEAD
(made in one piece)
Using 2.75mm needles and A, cast on 20 sts.

Row 1: K each st tbl.
Row 2: P to end.
Row 3: K to end.
Row 4: P to end.
Row 5: K1, (yfwd, k2tog) 9 times, k1.
Beg with a p row, work 23 rows in stocking stitch.
Row 29: K4, [(k2tog) twice, k4] twice (16 sts).
Row 30: P to end; cut A and join in B.
Row 31: Using B, k to end.
Row 32: P to end.
Row 33: K6, (inc1 in next st) 4 times, k6 (20 sts).
Beg with a p row, work 5 rows in stocking stitch.
Row 39: K9, (inc1 in next st) twice, k9 (22 sts).

Row 40: P to end.
Row 41: K9, sl1, k1, psso, k2tog, k9 (20 sts).
Beg with a p row, work 3 rows in stocking stitch.
Row 45: (K2tog) 10 times (10 sts).
Row 46: (P2tog) 5 times (5 sts); cut yarn and thread through rem 5 sts.

SKIRT
Using 2.75mm needles and C, cast on 40 sts.
Row 1: K each st tbl.
Row 2: P to end.
Row 3: K to end.
Row 4: P to end.
Row 5: K1, (yfwd, k2tog) 19 times, k1.
Row 6: P to end.
Row 7: K to end; do not cut C but join in D.
Row 8: (P1D, 1C) to end of row; cut yarn D.

Beg with a k row, work 10 rows in stocking stitch.

Row 19: (K2tog) 20 times (20 sts).

Row 20: P to end.

Row 21: K to end.

Cast off knitwise.

ARMS AND SLEEVES
(make 2)

Using 2.75mm needles and B, cast on 4 sts.

Row 1: Inc1 in each st (8 sts).

Beg with a p row, work 3 rows in stocking stitch; cut B and join in A.

Using A, work 2 rows in stocking stitch; cut A and join in C.

Using C, work 6 rows in stocking stitch.

Row 13: Inc1 in each st (16 sts).

Beg with a p row, work 3 rows in stocking stitch.

Row 17: (K2tog) 8 times (8 sts).

Cast off purlwise.

COLLAR

Using 2.75mm needles and C, cast on 40 sts.

Row 1: K each st tbl.

Row 2: P to end.

Cast off knitwise.

CROWN

Using 2.25mm needles and E, cast on 22 sts.

Row 1: K each st tbl.

Rows 2–3: K to end.

Cast off knitwise.

BELT

Using 2.25mm needles and E, cast on 24 sts.

Cast off, knitting each st tbl.

MAKING UP

At base of body, fold first few rows to wrong side along eyelet row and stitch in place to create a picot hem. Stitch back seam of body and head. Run a length of yarn through the stitches at neckline, stuff head and draw up yarn to close opening and shape neck.

At the base of the skirt, fold first few rows to wrong side along eyelet row and stitch in place to create a picot hem. Stitch back seam of skirt; run a length of yarn through the stitches at waistline, slip on to body and stitch top of skirt to body at waistline, pulling up yarn to tighten top of skirt slightly. Stitch belt just below top of skirt, joining the ends at the back.

Stitch seams on each arm and sleeve piece, adding a little stuffing to them if you wish, and stitch tops of sleeves to sides of body. Place centre of cast-on edge of collar at centre back of neck, then bring ends of collar to front and tuck into top of waistband of skirt; stitch in place. Stitch button to centre front.

Cut strands of buttercup-yellow yarn, lay them across the top of the head and stitch in place down centre using matching yarn and backstitch. Join ends of crown to form a ring, then stitch this on top of head.

Use various colours of yarn to embroider features. For mouth, stitch a single horizontal stitch in pink, then couch with short vertical stitches. Stitch two horizontal short stitches in white for each eye, then, with blue yarn, stitch a small stitch vertically across the white strands. Outline the top of each eye in backstitch, and embroider pupils and nostrils using black embroidery thread. (See page 47 for more details about embroidering facial features.)

Captain Cutlass

Is he the terror of the oceans or simply a benign buccaneer?
Captain Constantine Cutlass, 'Tiny' to his friends,
is ready to take you on a pirate adventure.

MATERIALS

- 4-ply knitting yarn in Prussian blue (A), geranium red (B), white (C), beige (D), plum (E), black (F) and gold (G), plus small amounts of pink and turquoise
- One 'diamond' button
- Pair of 2.75mm (UK12:US2) knitting needles
- Pair of 2.25mm (UK13:US1) knitting needles
- Tapestry needle
- Needle and thread
- Polyester toy stuffing

SIZE

The Captain's body measures approx 2½in (6.25cm) in length.

TENSION

See page 40.

BODY AND HEAD
(in one piece)

Using 2.25mm needles and A, cast on 24 sts.
Row 1: K to end.
Row 2: P to end.
Rows 3–4: K to end.
Row 5: (K1, p1) 12 times.
Rep row 5 11 times more.
Cut yarn A and join in B; change to 2.75mm needles.

Sash

Using B and beg with a k row, work 4 rows in stocking stitch; cut yarn B and join in C.

Torso and head

Using C and beg with a k row, work 8 rows in stocking stitch.
Row 29: K1, k2tog, (k2, k2tog) 5 times, k1 (18 sts).
Row 30: P to end; cut yarn C and join in D.
Row 31: Using D, k to end.
Row 32: P to end.
Row 33: K1, inc1, (k2, inc1) 5 times, k1 (24 sts).
Beg with a p row, work 11 rows in stocking stitch.
Row 45: (K2tog) 12 times (12 sts).
Row 46: (P2tog) 6 times.
Cut yarn and thread through rem 6 sts.

ARMS
(make 2)

Using 2.75mm needles and D, cast on 4 sts.
Row 1: K to end.
Row 2: P to end.
Row 3: Inc1 in each st (8 sts).
Row 4: P to end.
Row 5: K to end.
Row 6: P to end; cut D and join in C.
Rows 7–9: Using D, k to end.
Beg with a p row, work 15 rows in stocking stitch.
Cast off.

JACKET

Main part

Using 2.75mm needles and E, cast on 28 sts.

Row 1 (WS): K each st tbl.

Row 2: K to end.

Row 3: K1, p to last st, k1.

Rep rows 2 and 3 eight times more.

Row 20: K4, [(k2tog) twice, k4] 3 times (22 sts).

Row 21: P to end.

Row 22: (K2tog) 11 times (11 sts).

Row 23: P to end.

Cast off.

SLEEVES
(make 2)

Using 2.75mm needles and E, cast on 11 sts.

Row 1 (WS): K each st tbl.

Row 2: K to end.

Beg with a p row, work 11 rows in stocking stitch.

Row 14: K1, sl1, k1, psso, k5, k2tog, k1 (9 sts).

Row 15: P to end.

Row 16: K1, sl1, k1, psso, k3, k2tog, k1 (7 sts).

Row 17: P to end.

Cast off.

COLLAR

Using 2.75mm needles and C, cast on 12 sts.

Row 1: K to end.

Row 2: Inc1 in first st, k10, inc1 in last st (14 sts).

Cast off.

HAT
(made in two pieces)
Crown

Using 2.25mm needles and F, cast on 1 st and k into front, back, front, back and front of this st (5 sts).

Row 1: Inc1 in each st (10 sts).

Row 2: P to end.

Row 3: (K1, inc1) 5 times (15 sts).

Row 4: P to end.

Row 5: (K2, inc1) 5 times (20 sts).

Row 6: P to end.

Row 7: (K3, inc1) 5 times (25 sts).

Row 8: P to end.

Row 9: K to end.

Cast off knitwise.

Brim

Cast on 5 sts.

Knit 68 rows. Cast off.

CUFF BANDS
(make 2)

Using 2.25mm needles and G, cast on 14 sts.

Row 1: K each st tbl.

Cast off.

COAT FASTENINGS
(make 2)

Using 2.25mm needles and G, cast on 5 sts.

Row 1: K each st tbl.

Cast off.

NOSE

Using 2.25mm needles and D, cast on 5 sts.

Beg with a k row, work 6 rows in stocking stitch.

Cast off.

EYE PATCH

Using 2.25mm needles and F, cast on 3 sts.

Row 1: K each st tbl.

Row 2: K to end.

Row 3: Sl1, k2tog, psso.

Cast off.

MAKING UP

At base of body, fold first few rows to wrong side along purl ridge and stitch in place to create a hem. Stitch back seam of body and head. Run a length of yarn through the stitches at neckline, stuff head and draw up yarn to close opening and shape neck.

Wrap jacket around body, placing the two side edges at centre front. Stitch about 1/2in (1cm) of these edges together, starting about 2 rows down from cast-off edge, and stitch coat fastenings across this join. Fold back edges below this point and stitch in place to form coat tails, then stitch cast-on edge of collar in place on top edge of jacket, around back of neck, and stitch collar points to front of jacket. Use a needle and thread to stitch button in centre of sash.

Stitch arm seams, stuffing with any yarn ends, then attach to top of main piece of jacket at shoulders. Stitch sleeve seams, slip each one over one of the arms and stitch in place, allowing the white purl ridge to show just below the jacket cuff. Stitch a cuff band on both cuffs, just above garter-stitch ridge.

Stitch seam on crown of hat and sew to top of head. Then stitch two short ends of hat brim together, run a gathering stitch around one long edge and pull up to fit head; stitch in place around bottom edge of crown; fold back brim at front and back. Make a small plume of turquoise yarn and stitch to one side of hat.

Create ears using beige yarn and bullion stitch. For nose, roll up, tucking in the cast-off edge and creating a tight cone with one end slightly thicker than the other. Stitch in place using tail of yarn, with thicker part at the base. Stitch eye patch in place and use yarn F to embroider a cord, an eye, a little moustache and a beard. Sew two small horizontal stitches for the mouth. (See page 47 for more details about embroidering facial features.)

Techniques

GETTING STARTED

YARNS

All the projects in this book have been made using four-ply yarn. I prefer to use natural fibres in my knitting projects, particularly pure wool, as it has a natural elasticity – but in some cases I have had to use man-made fibres and various blends in order to source suitable colours. You will need very small quantities of yarn for these little puppets, so before you go shopping for yarns, experiment with any oddments you already have, or shop online for bags containing mixed colours in small amounts.

NEEDLES

Only two different needle sizes have been used throughout this book: 2.75mm (UK12:US2) and 2.25mm (UK13:US1). These are smaller than you might expect in order to produce a firm, close-knit fabric that will hold its shape and not allow any stuffing to poke through. You will need one pair of each size and double-pointed versions for just a few of the component pieces that are knitted in the round. Two double-pointed needles are used to knit i-cords.

STUFFING

The puppets' heads are usually stuffed to give a firm result – and so is the Pig's body cavity. Use any commercial brand of toy stuffing for this, or save all the yarn ends you snip off and use these as padding.

FOLLOWING PATTERNS

Before you embark on any project, make sure you have all the tools and materials you require, then read through the pattern from beginning to end to make sure you understand it. Abbreviations are shown on page 48.

TENSION GUIDE

Most of the component parts for the puppets in this book are knitted to a similar tension (or gauge) – 15 sts and 20 rows to 2in (5cm), measured over stocking stitch on 2.75mm (UK12:US2) needles, using four-ply yarn. The smaller needles are sometimes used to produce an even firmer result on some of the smaller items such as hats and belts.

To check if your tension matches, work a swatch using four-ply yarn on 2.75mm (UK12:US2) needles and measure it. If you have more than 15 stitches over 2in (5cm), this indicates that you knit more tightly than the stated tension and your puppet is likely to end up smaller than the one in the picture, so you may wish to use a larger needle. If you have fewer stitches, you tend to knit more loosely, so choose a smaller needle. The exact tension is not critical, however, as long as you create a firm fabric that holds its shape and doesn't allow bits of stuffing to poke through.

Knitting know-how

SIMPLE CAST-ON

This is the main method used throughout the book; some knitters know it as 'two-needle' or 'chain' cast-on.

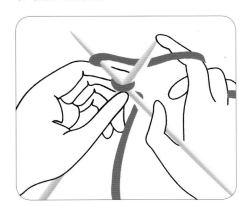

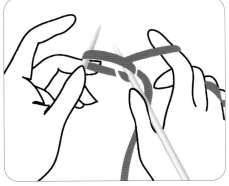

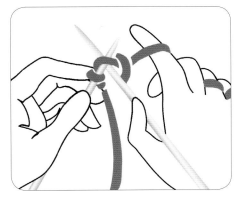

1 Make a slip knot and place it on the left-hand needle. *Insert the right-hand needle into the back of the loop, behind the left-hand needle, and wrap the yarn around it.

2 Use the right-hand needle to pull the yarn through the first loop, creating a new stitch.

3 Transfer this stitch to the left-hand needle and repeat from * until you have the required number of stitches.

CABLE CAST-ON

This creates a firm edge and can be used as the initial cast-on method or when casting on extra stitches further on in a pattern.

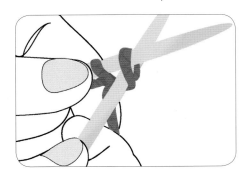

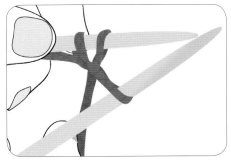

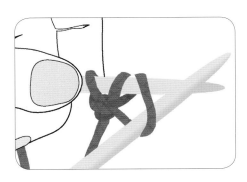

1 Make a slip knot and place it on the left-hand needle. Make one stitch using the simple cast-on method. *For the next stitch, insert the needle between the two stitches on the left-hand needle.

2 Wrap the yarn round the right-hand needle tip and pull through, between the previous two stitches.

3 Transfer the stitch you have made to the left-hand needle and repeat from * until you have the required number of stitches.

KNIT STITCH

1 To make a knit stitch, insert the tip of the right-hand needle into the next loop, and behind the left-hand needle, and wrap the yarn around it.

2 Use the right-hand needle to pull the yarn through the first loop, creating a new stitch.

3 Keep this new stitch on the right-hand needle and continue along the row.

PURL STITCH

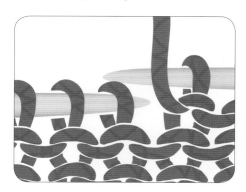 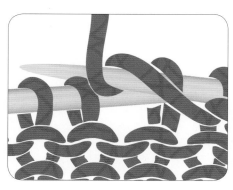 

1 To make a purl stitch, begin with the yarn at the front of the work.

2 Insert the tip of the right-hand needle into the front of the next loop, in front of the left-hand needle, and wrap the yarn around it.

3 Use the right-hand needle to pull the yarn through the first loop, creating a new stitch; keep this new stitch on the right-hand needle and continue along the row.

OTHER TYPES OF STITCHES

Rows of knit stitches produce a garter-stitch fabric (A); alternating rows of knit and purl stitches produce a stocking-stitch fabric (B) – but when knitting in the round, for stocking stitch you use only knit stitches. Alternating knit and purl stitches along a row produces textured effects, including ribbing (C) and moss stitch (D).

A   B   C   D

CASTING OFF

This is usually done using knit stitches – but occasionally you will be required to cast off in purl. To avoid confusion, and make it clear which method to use, the pattern instructions will, if necessary, tell you to cast off 'knitwise' or 'purlwise'. Where you are making a ribbed fabric, the instructions will usually tell you to cast off 'in rib' or 'ribwise'.

1 Knit the first two stitches on to the right-hand needle then, using the tip of the left-hand needle, slip the first stitch over the second stitch, leaving just one stitch on the needle.

2 Knit another stitch so that there are two stitches on the right-hand needle, and repeat the process until there is only one stitch left. Cut the yarn and thread the end of the yarn through the remaining stitch to fasten off.

SHAPING

The basic finger puppet consists of a tube of knitting that slips over the finger – but to create shoulders, heads and arms, and clothing such as jackets, skirts and hats, you need to shape some of the component parts.

Increasing

Increases are worked by casting on extra stitches at the beginning of a row, or by knitting into an existing stitch twice or three times. Where the pattern states 'inc 1', knit into the front and back of the stitch, thereby creating one extra stitch. Where the pattern states 'inc 2', knit into the front, the back and the front again, creating two extra stitches.

Decreasing

Decreases are worked in a number of different ways.

K2tog: Insert the right-hand needle into the front loops of the next two stitches and knit both stitches together.

K2tog tbl: Insert the right-hand needle into the back loops of the next two stitches and knit both stitches together.

K1, s1, psso: Slip the next stitch on to the right-hand needle, knit the next stitch, then using the tip of the left-hand needle, slip the slipped stitch over the knitted stitch.

P2tog: With the yarn at the front of the work, insert the right-hand needle into the front loops of the next two stitches and purl both stitches together.

P3tog: With the yarn at the front of the work, insert the right-hand needle into the front loops of the next three stitches and purl all three stitches together.

KNITTING IN THE ROUND

Most of the knitted components needed to make up each finger puppet are knitted flat, using two needles, and then stitched together to create three-dimensional shapes. A few of the components, however, are knitted 'in the round' on four needles. Knitting on four needles can be tricky, especially when you are working the first few rows. To cast on, use the two-needle 'simple' method, as it will create a firm, tight edge that is less likely to slip off the needles. For most of the patterns, you will see that the first row (or round) is knitted by inserting the needle into the back loop of each stitch, which also helps to form a firm edge.

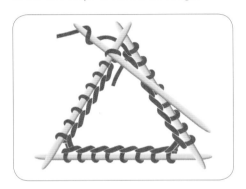

SINGLE-ROW STRIPES

This technique is used to make the Ringmaster's trousers. Normally when working in stocking stitch, to work single-row stripes you would have to cut the yarn at the end of each row and rejoin it, creating lots of yarn ends to darn in. This method uses two double-pointed needles removing the need to keep cutting the yarns.

Row 1: Cast on in yarn A; using B, k to end; do not cut B but slide sts to other end of needle and pick up A.
Row 2: Using A, k to end; turn work, pick up B and p to end of row using B.
Row 3: Slide sts to other end of needle, pick up A and p to end of row; turn.
Row 4: Using B, k to end.
Continue in this way, working single rows in alternate colours until the desired number of rows have been worked.

Making Up

When working on such a small scale, the aim is to be as neat as possible. When joining the sides of two knitted pieces, it is advisable to use one of two methods: mattress stitch or backstitch. When joining two straight edges – usually a cast-on edge to a cast-off edge – oversew the edges for a neat result. This method would be used when wrapping a small strip of knitting around a plastic straw to make the Ringmaster's whip or the Witch's broom, for example. You may also find overstitching the easiest and neatest way to stitch the cast-off row at the top of an arm or sleeve to a body.

OVERSEWING

Line up the edges to be joined and whipstitch together on the right side of the work.

MATTRESS-STITCH SEAM

This method creates an invisible seam.

1 Thread a blunt needle with a long length of matching yarn. With the right side of the work facing, place the two edges together.

2 Starting at the bottom edge of the work, insert the needle under the bar between the first and second stitches on the right-hand side.

3 Insert the needle in the same way on the opposite edge.

4 Repeat, working across from left to right and back again, moving up the seam. Do not pull stitches tight.

5 When you reach the top of the seam, pull the yarn ends until the two sides meet; do not pull too tightly or you will cause the seam to pucker. Fasten off yarn ends securely.

BACKSTITCH SEAM

This method creates an invisible seam.

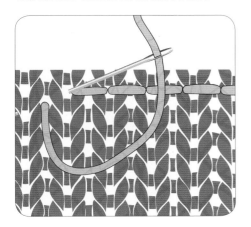

1 Thread a blunt needle with a long length of matching yarn. Place the two pieces to be joined on top of one another, right sides together.

2 Working from right to left, one stitch in from selvedge, bring the needle up through both layers then back down through both layers one row to the left.

3 Bring the needle back up through both layers one row to the left, then back down one row to the right, in the same place as before.

4 Repeat, taking the needle two rows to the left each time, and one row back.

GATHERING
(EDGES)

To gather a cast-on or cast-off edge, thread the tail of yarn into a blunt needle and run the needle through each stitch on that edge, then pull up. If you are closing the hole at the top of a head, for example, run the needle through the stitches a second time and pull up tightly to close the hole, then fasten off the end of the yarn firmly and trim off any excess.

GATHERING
(SHAPING)

To gather stitches in the centre of a piece of work – for example, when you are forming a neck between body and head – stitch a running stitch through the stitches of a single row, using matching yarn, then pull up to the required width.

MAKING AN I-CORD

The i-cord is a knitted cord that can be made up of two or more stitches. In this book, i-cords are used in various ways – to make arms for the Monkey, for example, and to roll up to form the Frog's eyes.

Using two double-pointed needles, cast on the required number of stitches and knit all stitches. Do not turn the work but slide the stitches to the opposite end of the right-hand needle, transfer this needle to the other hand and, taking the yarn firmly across the back of the work, knit the stitches. Repeat the process until the cord is the desired length.

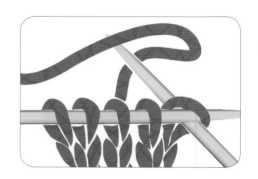

Finishing off

There is more to making a finger puppet than simply knitting the component parts and stitching them together. It is not always easy, when working on such a small scale, to add a lot of detail, but there is scope for creativity. With a few deft stitches, you can alter the angle of a head or the positioning of arms, for example. Even the placement of a hat can make subtle changes to your puppet's demeanour.

HAIR

1 Some of the finger puppets in this book have stitched-on hair using satin stitch, while some have more complex hairstyles. Follow the instructions given for each finger puppet or customize the characters by choosing your own hairstyle.

2 To create bushy hair, make a bundle of yarn by wrapping yarn around two or more fingers, then tie firmly around the centre. Stitch the centre of the bundle to the head. If the puppet has a hat or scarf, stitch this in place on top of the hair before trimming the ends of the yarn to create a 'hairstyle'. Experiment with different ways of attaching the bundle until you find a method that suits you. For example, if you tie the bundle of threads quite loosely, you can spread it out across the top and the back of the head and couch the central length of yarn in place from the centre front to the nape of the neck to form a centre parting – ideal if you wish to make a hairstyle that involves plaits or bunches at each side.

3 For wispy hair, separate the strands of thread by running a blunt needle from the top of each strand, where it emerges from the head or the hat brim, to the tip. Trim yarn ends to the desired length.